Hibernation

Anita Ga

Heinemann
LIBRARY

Young Explorer

www.heinemann.co.uk/library
Visit our website to find out more information about **Heinemann Library** books.

To order:
☎ Phone 44 (0) 1865 888066
🖷 Send a fax to 44 (0) 1865 314091
🖳 Visit the Heinemann Bookshop at www.heinemann.co.uk/library to browse our catalogue and order online.

First published in Great Britain by Heinemann Library, Halley Court, Jordan Hill, Oxford OX2 8EJ, part of Harcourt Education. Heinemann is a registered trademark of Harcourt Education Ltd.

Editorial: Jilly Attwood, Kate Bellamy
Design: Jo Hinton-Malivoire
Picture research: Kay Altwegg, Ruth Blair
Production: Séverine Ribierre

Originated by Dot Gradations Ltd
Printed and bound in China by South China Printing Company

ISBN 0 431 11409 9 (hardback)
09 08 07 06 05
10 9 8 7 6 5 4 3 2 1

ISBN 0 431 11415 3 (paperback)
10 09 08 07 06
10 9 8 7 6 5 4 3 2 1

British Library Cataloguing in Publication Data
Ganeri, Anita
Hibernation – (Nature's Patterns)
591.5'65
A full catalogue record for this book is available from the British Library.

Acknowledgements
The Publishers would like to thank the following for permission to reproduce photographs: Corbis pp. **10**, **14**; Corbis pp. **6** (Peter Johnson), **24** (George D Lepp), **9** (Kennan Ward); Nature Photo Library pp. **27** (Alfo), **19** (Ingo Arndt), **25** (Asgeir Helgestad), **17** (Paul Hobson), **4** (George McCarthy), **26** (Steven David Miller), **5** (David Tipling); NHPA pp. **21** (Anthony Bannister), **13** (Daniel Heuclin), **28** (V Hurst and T Kitchin), **11** (Rich Kirchner), **18** (Eric Soder), **22** (Robert Thompson); OFS pp. **7**, **8**, **12**, **15**, **16**, **20**, **23**, **29**.

Cover photograph of a dormouse hibernating is reproduced with permission of Nature Photo Library.

Our thanks to David Lewin for his assistance in the preparation of this book.

Contents

Words appearing in the text in bold, **like this**, are explained in the Glossary.

 Find out more about Nature's Patterns at www.heinemannexplore.co.uk

Nature's patterns

Nature is always changing. Many of the changes that happen follow a **pattern**. This means that they happen over and over again.

This sleeping dormouse will wake up in spring.

The poorwill, from North America, is the only bird that hibernates.

Hibernation is like a very deep sleep. It is a pattern that usually happens each year. Many animals hibernate at the beginning of winter. Then they wake up again in spring.

Winter sleep

Winter is a hard time for animals. The weather can be very cold and there is not much food to eat. Some animals have to **hibernate** to stay alive.

These ground squirrels sleep right through winter.

Sometimes bears wake up to eat during their long sleep.

Some animals sleep very deeply when they hibernate. They hardly breathe and their heart beats very slowly. Other animals doze off but they wake up from time to time.

Storing fat

An Alpine **marmot** eats lots of seeds before it hibernates.

In summer, animals get ready to **hibernate**. Some animals eat a lot of extra food and get very fat. In winter, they use this store of fat to stay alive.

A brown bear gathers berries ready for winter.

Animals like bears collect lots of fruit, nuts and berries. They hide this food in their **burrows** or **dens**. They snack on it during the winter.

A place to sleep

Animals must find a safe place to sleep. Some animals dig **dens** and **burrows**. Others look for caves and hollow trees. Some animals **hibernate** under stones or piles of leaves.

Polar bears dig their dens in the snow.

In autumn, animals get their sleeping places ready. Some animals collect grass and leaves to put in their burrows. This helps to keep them warm in winter.

Marmots *line their burrows with soft grass.*

Settling down

Some animals **hibernate** on their own. They hide away in a hole or **den** and quickly fall asleep. A toadfish digs a **burrow** in the mud on the sea bed.

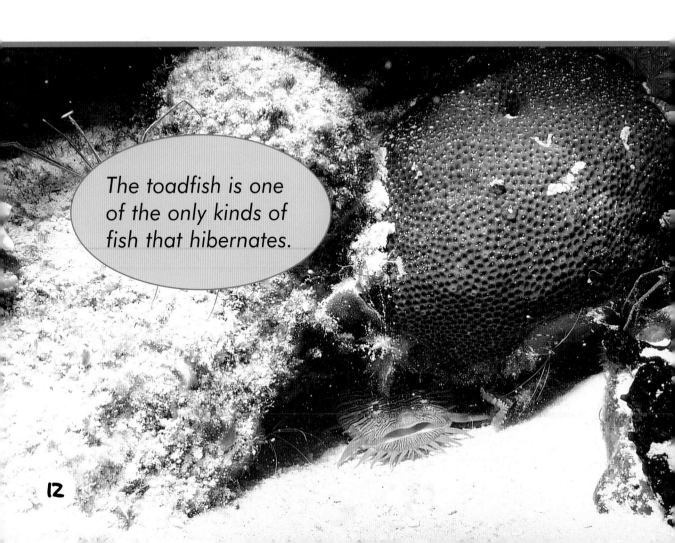

The toadfish is one of the only kinds of fish that hibernates.

Animals, like bats, snakes and butterflies, hibernate in big groups. This is so they can huddle together and stay warm.

Rattlesnakes sometimes hibernate in groups.

Slowing down

When an animal **hibernates**, it falls into a deep sleep. Its body works more slowly than normal. Its heart beats very slowly and its breathing slows right down.

A woodchuck's body works very slowly while it is asleep.

An animal's body gets very cold because its **temperature** drops. All of these changes help the animal to save **energy** until it wakes up in spring.

A hibernating bat can get so cold that ice sticks to its body.

Food and waste

Some animals sleep right through the winter. They do not eat anything. Other animals do not sleep so deeply.

Chipmunks wake up to eat food they have stored in their **burrows**.

Animals, like hedgehogs, wake up every few weeks. They have something to eat or drink and they go to the toilet. Then they go back to sleep.

Hedgehogs leave their **dens** to eat.

Sleepyheads

Some **hibernating** animals go to sleep almost as soon as the cold weather begins. Others go through a sleepy time before they finally fall asleep.

Fire salamanders become sleepy during the winter.

Alpine marmots sleep for months when they hibernate.

Some animals stay asleep for a few months. Others only sleep for a few weeks. Alpine **marmots** are real sleepyheads. They can sleep for more than six months.

19

Waking Up

When spring comes, the **hibernating** animals start to wake up. They know that it is time to wake up because the weather gets warmer.

A groundhog leaves its **burrow** in the spring.

A toad comes out of its winter burrow in the mud.

The animals have to wake up very slowly otherwise they might die. Their bodies begin to warm up and they start to move about.

A good meal

Many **hibernating** animals do not eat very much. They live off fat in their bodies or small stores of food in their **dens**. They lose a lot of weight while they are asleep.

When butterflies wake up in spring, they need to find flowers to feed on.

In the spring, there are berries and fruit to feed on.

When animals wake up in the spring, they are thin and hungry. But there is a lot of food around and they can have a good meal.

Having babies

In spring, the weather is warm and there is a lot of food to eat. This makes it a good time for many animals to have their babies.

Some animals start to build their nests as soon as they wake up.

There is plenty of food in spring and summer for bear cubs to eat.

Animals, like bears, have their babies in their winter **dens**. They **nurse** them through the winter. In spring, the mother bear leaves the den with her **cubs**.

25

Back to sleep

In autumn, the weather gets cooler and it gets darker earlier in the evening. When this happens, animals know that it is time to get ready to **hibernate** again.

A terrapin goes into its **burrow**, ready to hibernate.

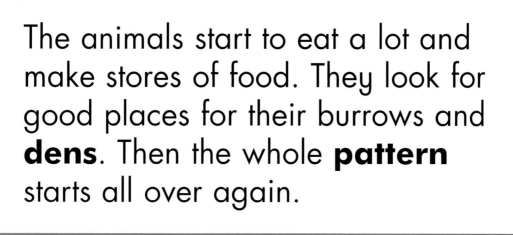

The animals start to eat a lot and make stores of food. They look for good places for their burrows and **dens**. Then the whole **pattern** starts all over again.

A golden hamster finds a cosy bed among the leaves.

Cooling down

In hot places, some animals hide away and sleep when the weather gets very warm and dry. This is a bit like **hibernation** but it is not the same thing.

Desert toads sleep during the very warm, dry weather.

A desert frog sleeps in an underground **burrow** where it is much cooler.

The animals wake up when it starts to rain or when the weather gets cooler. When the weather turns hot and dry, the **pattern** starts all over again.

fact file

- Arctic ground squirrels in North America hold the world record for **hibernating**. They sleep for eight months a year.

- Some hibernating bats only breathe once every two hours.

- Terrapins hibernate in the mud at the bottom of a pond. They stay alive by breathing air trapped inside their shells.

Find out more about Nature's Patterns at www.heinemannexplore.co.uk

Glossary

burrow a hole that an animal makes in the ground

cub young bear

den place, like a cave, where animals can live

energy strength which is made by eating food

hibernate to go into a deep sleep during the winter

marmot a kind of small, furry animal

nurse to feed and look after a baby animal

pattern something that happens over and over again

temperature how hot or cold something is

More books to read

Amazing Nature: Hidden Hibernators, Malcolm Penny (Heinemann Library, 2004)

A Bed for Winter, Karen Wallace (Dorling Kindersley, 2000)

Hibernation (Circle of Life), Carolyn Scrace (Franklin Watts, 2002)

Index